Acquainted with Grief
Words of Comfort from a Brother

Michael Wyatt

with

Joyce Cope Wyatt

The Publishing Group @ Parsons Porch

Acquainted with Grief
Words of Comfort from a Brother

Michael Wyatt

with

Joyce Cope Wyatt

Parson's Porch Books

A cquainted with Grief

ISBN: Softcover 978-1-936912-64-3

Copyright © 2012 by Joyce Cope Wyatt

To order additional copies of this book, contact:

Parson's Porch Books

1-423-475-7308

www.parsonsporchbooks.com

Parson's Porch Books is an imprint of Parson's Porch & Company (PP&C) in Cleveland, Tennessee. PP&C is an innovative non-profit organization which raises money to help people in trouble by publishing books of noted authors, representing all genres. All profits are shared with Parson's Porch.

TABLE OF CONTENTS

Preface   **11**

Author's Note   **15**

Letters from Michael to Kathryn   **17**

Post Data - Letter from Michael to Kathryn's Family   **63**

Michael's Eulogy of Kathryn   **65**

Letter from Michael to Kathryn about   **69**
     What it was like to be in a Coma

Remembrance of Michael   **75**

Kathryn Annis Wyatt Mee

PREFACE

On October 29, 1998, we found out that our daughter Kathryn had a brain tumor. She had given birth to her seventh child, Karen, just five weeks before. While she had been having some signs of problems during the final month of her pregnancy, she and others attributed it to the stress of giving birth to a seventh child. However, the MRI confirmed that there was another cause, a tumor in the brain, over the left ear. The next day began consultations with neurosurgeons, oncologists, and other medical personnel. Surgery came the following week, with the breath-taking diagnosis, a glioblastoma multiforme grade four tumor, and the most virulent of brain tumors. At 44 years of age she was told that the average prognosis was a life expectancy of 42 weeks!

From the first Kathryn's faith in God gave her both a will to live and the strength to undergo whatever treatment might give her added years of life. She kept a picture of the family with her husband and all seven children nearby to show her doctors and those who cared for her that she needed to live for her family. From time to time when she would admit to fatigue she told me that when she would bend over to pick up something from the floor, she would have liked to have been able just to lie down and rest, "but the children" needed her. Her response to that need kept her going in spite of fatigue. She walked daily to keep up her energy; she tried all sorts of food combinations, limiting her diet of foods that she felt would be harmful to her body and adding others that might give some benefit. She underwent five craniotomies and an additional surgery to remove an area of infection in the skull, followed by plastic surgery. She had radiation, chemotherapy and additional experimental chemotherapies. The prayers and loving concern of people everywhere were a constant encouragement to her. She had time and energy to give to her family and to the many who loved being around her, for she was a constant witness to God's love and abounding care.

Suddenly in January of 2000 her brother Michael was stricken with bacterial meningitis, and we were told that he was dying in a hospital in Sheldon, Washington, the area where he had been visiting friends. Roy and I flew to Washington to be with him the following day, and slowly Michael began to improve. The pain and suffering he was experiencing were evident, but again his faith and the prayers of so many gave him hope and strength for the long process of healing. His "acquaintance with grief and suffering" in this excruciating experience gave him a rapport with Kathryn that went beyond the love of brother and sister. His own near-death experience enabled him to understand her needs, her fears, her grief, and gave her special comfort in his words. "How he has ministered to our family," she told me.

These two illnesses had brought our family closer together, and both Michael, who now lives in Washington, D. C., and Debbie, our youngest child who lives in Canada, came to be with Kathryn as frequently as possible for brief or more extended visits. Christmas of 2002 we were together as a family. It was obvious that Kathryn was growing weaker, and abruptly in early January she gave evidences of even further debilitation.

Both Michael and Debbi planned to visit in late February. Kathryn was now confined to the bed. Debbi had to cancel her plans because of the illness of her small son, but Michael was able to be with Kathryn and us for three days. During that time he read to her from the Bible - passages which she loved and had memorized, but could no longer remember. In his words, "The Bible became, in a sense, fresh to her again. Scripture took on new depth. She was hearing as if for the first time the reassurances of the God she trusted, and she recognized, if not the words, the love. She would sit in her chair, and later lie in her bed, and she would echo some of the words, or say "Oh, yes," or "thank you." As speaking became more difficult, she would simply make little sounds of appreciation and gratitude, as if listening to the words of a love-letter."

Knowing that he could not be here every day to read to her, Michael began to send a daily card to her in which he had copied words of Scripture followed by a brief meditation. They arrived daily, written on beautiful scenes from The National Cathedral, of paintings from the great museums of the world. Kathryn, who loved beauty, would reach out to touch them, to receive the blessing of such beauty, and to hear the blessing of the comforting words they contained.

There were 46 cards which brought those blessings – one each day. As we read them to Kathryn we realized that we were being blessed and comforted, too. And if they spoke so meaningfully both to Kathryn's needs and to our needs during the period prior to her death surely they would bring blessing, comfort and insight for others who would share this same path. And so, the idea of publishing them and making them available to whomever might need to hear that message was born. Michael has given his permission; however he has assured me that these messages were written for Kathryn, not with the idea of their publication. However, if they can bring comfort and blessing to others, both he and Kathryn would be pleased and would give glory to God.

Kathryn died on March 26. Her death was peaceful. She is with the Lord.

Our prayer is that this book and its profound message of comfort may be a blessing to all who read it.

Joyce Cope Wyatt

AUTHOR'S NOTE

In sending these selections of Scripture with their brief reflections, I was informed by the practice in many religions of reading sacred texts to a person on their deathbed as a guide through the process of dying. What mattered most to me was to offer something genuinely needed and desired. I knew that my sister built her life on Scripture and had asked me to read Scripture to her, and I knew that she had asked me about my own near-death experience. There I had the two requests that she had made of me. I simply trusted that the verses that came to me each morning were the right ones to send that day, and I trusted that, as I stilled myself in the presence of those verses and thought of what had helped me, the words I wrote would be the right words.

Michael Wyatt

1

Dearest Kathryn –

> *Those who wait for the Lord shall renew their strength, they*
> *shall mount up with wings like eagles, they shall run and*
> *not be weary, and they shall walk and not faint.*
>
> *Isaiah 40:31*

This promise is true because Christ dwells within us. The strength is not given to us in small amounts from the outside, but opens up inside us, as a wellspring we cannot exhaust. Christ in you does not run dry, even if you send the bucket down for grace deeper and deeper each day. The water table of God runs under everything, under every moment of life - it's always there.

I love you and pray for you, Michael

2

Dearest Kathryn –

Jesus himself came near and went with them, but their eyes were kept from recognizing him.   Luke 24:15-16

These disciples were mourning the death of Jesus; everything they cared for and all they hoped for had been torn from them. And yet, walking next to them, unknown to them, unseen by them, was everything they loved, restored to them more gloriously.

We cannot always perceive the hope we lean on to steady us as we go forward. But all along, God walks next to us, asking us to show Him our troubles, willing to wait as we unburden ourselves. Sometimes we do not perceive He is there at all, except that our peace increases and our praise becomes something we observe and describe to ourselves; and we realize that even our deepest grief, He is already familiar with.

I love you and pray for you daily, Michael.

3

Dearest Kathryn –

> *Lord, you have been our dwelling place in all generations.*
> *Psalm 90:1*

Sickness shows us where we dwell. Because I could not get away from my body when I was sick, I learned more deeply than before that I am made dwelling in a body. We human beings are built to be humble, not shamed, before God and each other, and our helplessness in our body shows us that.

But the patience we must learn in order to love our flesh and forgive ourselves for being mortal has no other dwelling place than our faith in God. When I was sick, not only did I not rise or sink away from my body, but my presence in my body became for me the picture of God's presence in my life. Just as I watched my suffering, so God watched me. Just as I found myself in my body, so I found God in me. That, by God's grace in Christ, is the secure dwelling place of both painful body and patient soul.

I love you and pray for you daily, Michael

4

Dearest Kathryn –

> *God made the storm be still and the waves of the sea were hushed. Then they were glad because they had quiet, and he brought them to their desired haven. Psalm 107:29-30*

Because God is everywhere, we are at every moment close to our safe haven. Physical pain can be a violent storm to us, but as the depth of our hearts reach God and touch Him; we are already brought to a protected harbor. We cannot want to go there more than our Lord wants to bring us there. We only need to hand over the steering of our soul to Him. When we suffer, our hands tremble, but His remain steady, beyond the spasms and jerks of our frightened mind and painful body. He is already in you, plotting the true course. Our work in sickness is to loosen, finger by finger, over and over, our grip, to let our heart be tender and open, and to hand things to Christ in trust over and over.

I love you and pray for you daily, Michael

5

Dearest Kathryn –

> *He will feed his flock like a shepherd; he will gather the*
> *lambs in his arms and carry them in his bosom, and gently*
> *lead the mother sheep. Isaiah 40:11*

When I think for how many years this verse has been both
a promise and a fulfillment for you, I want to use this note
to recall it with you. All of us have verses that are spoken
directly into our hearts; we can feel how our heart stirs and
turns to face God when we hear them. This is already the
verse coming true.

In these days, more and more, you will know its truth; you
will take your place in the flock being led home. God
leads the mother sheep gently, not because there is no pain
or heat or desert stretches, but because Christ does not
force himself on us. Sometimes, he walks behind us, but
we know he is there. But you, Kathryn, are also his own
lamb, and when you cannot lift yourself, he will gather you
in his arms, and carry you in his bosom. When you feel
you have no more strength, feel his arms beneath you,
gathering you up; then let yourself rest there.

I love you and pray for you daily, Michael

6

Dearest Kathryn –

> *Jesus took the five loaves and two fish, and looking up to heaven, he gave thanks and broke the loaves. Then he gave them to his disciples to set before the people. He also divided the two fish among them all. They all ate and were satisfied. Mark 6:41-42 (NIV)*

We recognize that God is present when we are satisfied, when the root of our soul is nourished, when our depth is at rest and content. When God is with us, even a fragment is enough. When God is absent, even banquets leave us famished. You and I know what it is to have a life in fragments.

I remember when I was sick, the sense that my life had been broken down into fragments, and reduced to essential pieces that couldn't fall apart any further: basic bodily functions, no more. Then, to sleep, to eat, to breathe – these were all I needed to do. Everything else, all my responsibilities, I had needed to hand over to others. Then, to be alone with the pain I was in and with the physical fragments of my life was a place to meet God. I learned that my breath – each and every breath – was good. I learned that my poor body, which I had ignored and abused, but which had served me faithfully for half a century, was good. I pitied my body's struggle to survive, and I felt compassion for it, and I wanted to provide for it. Each moment on its own satisfied me, because it was caring for my life, and I began to see that God was present in every breath, because every breath was a gift and satisfied me.

I love you and pray for you daily, Michael

7

Dearest Kathryn –

> *The good shepherd calls his own sheep by name and leads them out. John 10:3*

When the time comes to leave the safety of the fold, most of us need to follow a voice we recognize. When we are exhausted by illness and confused by the changes our body is going through, it can become hard to hear God's voice as we once did. But as we lose our habitual ways of hearing God, as we lose touch with the places we expect to meet Him, we find our self again at the moment of conversion, hearing God's voice in a new way, calling us to a new depth of trust.

God found us and called us by name when we did not know Him. When I was sick and hardly knew myself, God found me there also. And even though it was not a place where I had known God before, and even though I did not know how to be faithful when all my reliable strength was taken from me, I recognized the voice of God – strong and steady and loving – just as I recognized it as a child. The strange blessing of illness is that we are forced to trust – how wonderful that God meets us and calls us there! We only need to follow Him.

I love you and pray for you daily, Michael

8

Dearest Kathryn –

> *O Lord, you are my portion and my cup; it is you who upholds my lot. My boundaries enclose a pleasant land; indeed I have a goodly heritage. Psalm 16:5-6 (The Psalter, the Book of Common Prayer)*

Especially when we are sick, we come to understand that God truly is our portion. As other things fall away, God remains. As we lose strength and taste and capacity – all the ways we used to know pleasure – the pleasant land that is God-in-us remains. The boundaries of our soul enclose where we meet God; and, by the grace of Christ, that place where God dwells in us is our goodly heritage, our true possession. Everything else we move through as aliens and migrants; however dear it is to us, none of it is ours to keep. God may visit us there, but does not dwell there. The goodly land of our spirit, always ours because it is us, is the portion God has given us; and it is goodly because it can never be lost to us, the depth of our heart, where God has chosen to dwell, to strengthen us and bless us.

I love you and pray for you daily, Michael

9

Dearest Kathryn –

> *I will bless the Lord, who gives me counsel; my heart
> teaches me, night after night. I have set the Lord always
> before me; because he is at my right hand, I shall not fall.*
>
> *My heart, therefore, is glad, and my spirit rejoices; My body
> also shall rest in hope. Psalm 16:7-9 (The Psalter, The
> Book of Common Prayer)*

Only because Christ truly dwells in us can our heart teach
us in the night, when all other means of teaching are silent
or unseen. When we can do nothing else, we can still set
God before us. When I was unable to get out of bed when
I was sick, my friend Robin brought me an icon of Jesus
which we put on the wall in front of my bed. But that was
only the reminder that even in the dark I knew how to
keep my gaze turned on the image of Christ.

Recalling God's love in the dark, even when it is no more
than a memory of our heart's being broken open, even
when we are not sure of our full gratitude, lets our body
rest in hope. When nothing else is possible, because all
that is left to us in our night is our heart, when our heart
holds God, we rest in hope.

I love you and pray for you daily, Michael.

10

Dearest Kathryn –

> *You, O Lord, will not abandon me to the grave, nor let your holy one see the Pit. You will show me the path of life; in your presence there is fullness of joy, and in your right hand are pleasures for evermore. Psalm 16:10 and 11 (The Psalter, The Book of Common Prayer)*

Our footing on the path of life is given to us one step at a time. Especially being sick, I realized this: my attention and energy was brought in very close, to physical pain and physical needs. The large vision of faith fell away. So I came to see that what falls away could not be essential.

What was essential was shown to me to be this: God was present, holding me up, in everything necessary for me to do. Each step, because it required trust and because it was beyond my control, had to be surrendered to God. That is the path of life. Doing each necessary thing – the basic needs of our body – faithfully, knowing I can only do this because God sustains me, is to be in God's presence continually. Knowing God holds us each moment, we know we are not abandoned to our grave.

I love you and pray for you daily, Michael

11

Dearest Kathryn –

> *Thus says the Lord, who created you, O Jacob, and formed you, O Israel: "Do not fear, for I have redeemed you; I have called you by name, you are mine. When you pass through the waters, I will be with you, and through the rivers, they will not overwhelm you; when you walk through fire, you shall not be burned, and the flame shall not consume you." Isaiah 43:1-2*

In illness, we understand the truth of this. When I was sick, I felt at my worst that I was almost submerged, that I was sinking into water. Yet, I was aware and not afraid. The part of me that knew who I was remained intact. But I believe part of its remaining intact was becoming aware – not as an act of faith, but as a discovery – that God was present. I knew I was not alone because I was not afraid, but able to witness the pain I was in and even witness the loss of control and disintegration. It was like sitting on God's lap, for whom this illness was a moment and not what mattered. Even though it filled all my life at that moment, from one horizon to the other, even though I could not reach the edge of my sickness anywhere and could run nowhere to escape it, even when being sick flooded me with waters I couldn't resist, that overwhelmed me physically, still for God it was something to pass through. Collapsed as I was on God's lap, like a worn-out child, somehow I saw that my ability to see my illness, to watch it, was to begin to know it as God knows it: a huge river, but only a river, and passable. So in the midst of it all, I was at peace on God's lap even as I struggled, and overwhelmed, not consumed, even alone, not alone.

I love you and pray for you daily. Michael

12

Dearest Kathryn –

> *People were bringing little children to him in order that he might touch them; and the disciples spoke sternly to them. But when Jesus saw this, he was indignant and said to them, "Let the little children come to me; do not stop them; for it is to such as these that the Kingdom of God belongs. Truly, I tell you, whoever does not receive the Kingdom of God as a little child will never enter it." And he took them up in his arms, laid his hands on them, and blessed them. Mark 10:13-16*

Illness returns us to being children. We can no longer do what we wish or control what we want, and the world is full of people with more understanding and others who make decisions for us. Often we react with rage and fear. But I found that, beyond my ability, an opportunity was given in illness to reach the simplicity of the child, to deepen in trust and surrender, to discover trust because it was the truth of my physical condition. So, because we are back at our simplest life, our relation to God can simplify as well, coming to depend on those who read to us and pray for us and care for us. So we are brought to Jesus' lap, to his hands, tender and gentle, full of healing and blessing, to rest there, as a child would.

I love you and pray for you daily, Michael

13

Dearest Kathryn –

> *Deliver me, O Lord, by your hand from those whose portion in life is this world; whose bellies you fill with your treasure, who are well supplied with children and leave their wealth to their little ones. But at my vindication, I shall see your face; When I awake, I shall be satisfied, beholding your likeness. Psalm 17:14-15 (The Psalter, The Book of Common Prayer)*

You told me once these words mattered to you. Coming awake is seeing God's likeness everywhere. Seeing God's likeness everywhere is being awake. Even for those well supplied with children, what matters more is the satisfaction of beholding in them God's likeness. Even watching our own struggle to be faithful, which can be like the fitful effort of a nightmare when we are sick – climbing and not reaching, running and not escaping - we see moments of peace and wake into God's comfort and strength; then we see in us the likeness of Jesus, patient under suffering and know it is a gift from God, therefore another glimpse of God's likeness.

I love you and pray for you daily, Michael

14

Dearest Kathryn –

I will lift up my eyes to the hills; from where is my help to come? My help comes from the Lord, who made heaven and earth. He will not let your foot be moved and he who watches over you will not fall asleep; Behold, he who keeps watch over Israel shall neither slumber nor sleep. Psalm 121: 1-4 (The Psalter, The Book of Common Prayer)

Not only our health, but our faith and hope are in God's hands. When we have no strength of our own, we are sustained. What made the hills around us, made us. We do not go through anything unfamiliar to God or greater that He is.

Notice how your heart is unmoved in your love for your husband and children. Notice how your desire to honor Jesus remains unmoved. These unmovable pledges that you experience as yours are kept steady by God. Every morning we wake and our loyalties and loves are still there. In them, beneath them, never slumbering, keeping us steady, is God, who does not lose what is entrusted to Him

I love you and pray for you daily, Michael

15

Dearest Kathryn –

> *The Lord is your keeper; the Lord is your shade at your right hand. The sun shall not strike you by day, nor the moon by night. Psalm 121:5-6*

It is hard, when we feel we are being struck by pain constantly, to find where God shades us. When I was sick, the pain was overwhelming. But it was possible for me to find moments when I "noticed" the pain rather than suffer it, when I could watch was happening to me. These moments "happened" to me at first; but as soon as I caught, out of the corner of my eye, that this part of me was undisturbed and compassionate, I came to rely on it more. Of course, I could do nothing but endure the pain, but having noticed the part of me that was unaltered by the pain, the part of me that stayed the same; I tried to return there as I could.

This place, the core of our soul, is where God shades us and keeps us. We know we are there and that it is where God meets us, because the qualities of God surface in us: first of all, a loving gaze and compassion. In that sense, as we suffer, we can watch our pain with God, from that depth where we cannot be harmed.

I love you and pray for you daily, Michael.

16

Dearest Kathryn –

*The Lord will keep you from all evil; he will keep your life.
The Lord will watch over your going out and your coming
in. From this time forth and forever more. Psalm 121:7-8
(The Psalter, The Book of Common Prayer)*

Pain is not evil, nor is sickness, nor is death, because God
can come closer to us in all three. Our struggle against
them makes them seem so, because as we struggle, we can
think we are alone; then they do seem overwhelming. But
the same moment in which our soul sees that pain and
sickness and death cannot destroy it – the moment we are
freed to watch our pain – is the moment we can realize
that our soul is safe, because it is in God's hands, for
whom pain and sickness and death are no threat at all. So
it is true of all our coming and going; we cannot go further
than God. As we go out into sleep, or even as you have
gone out in seizures, God sustains your coming back in
and keeps your life, which He sees as precious and worth
watching over forever.

I love you and pray for you daily, Michael

17

Dearest Kathryn –

> *In Jesus Christ every one of God's promises is a "Yes."*
> *For this reason it is through him that we say "Amen," to*
> *the glory of God. II Corinthians 1:20*

On the day I was in the emergency room for meningitis, when I had already turned into dying, and the pain was so intense and my ability to respond destroyed, I recall no fear. My body was suffering, as it must. Our body was not made for us to keep. But I believe that somehow, without my knowing it, Jesus' "Yes" was preserving what is entrusted to him. I did not know it at the time, because the illness was so savage, and one is made very simple by sickness, reduced to essentials. But the comfort is that even when I couldn't put my faith into words, the action of faith – the trusting peaceful heart – I <u>discovered</u> I had in Christ, and through him could intend my "Amen."

I love you and pray for you daily, Michael

18

Dearest Kathryn –

The sea became rough, because a strong wind was blowing. When the disciples had rowed about three or four miles, they saw Jesus walking on the sea, and coming near the boat, and they were terrified... But he said to them, "It is I; do not be afraid." Then they wanted to take him into the boat. John 6:18-21

Even when we are tempest-tossed, Jesus' desire is to approach us, to reassure and encourage us. That can mean looking for his approach in a new place, in a new way, even a way that is frightening to us, because it means being open to an unfamiliar way of being with God.

But the sign of God's presence is always, "I am" and "do not be afraid." And in each of us, God moves saying, "I am what makes you you; I sustain the part of you that says 'I am;' I am why there is no reason to fear; I reside in the part of you, your deepest heart, where there is no fear, because I walk on those waters."

I love you and pray for you daily, Michael

19

Dearest Kathryn –

> *Taste and see that the Lord is good; happy are they who trust in him! Psalm 34:8 (The Psalter, The Book of Common Prayer)*

We cannot see or handle what we taste; in order to taste something, we must have it in us. God has, then, many blessings which are perceived only at the back of our throat, whose goodness we perceive only as we swallow them and take them in and make them part of us. Our task is to savor them, to notice and give thanks, when, during the course of the day, without our effort, we taste God. God feeds us with forgiveness and hope, with strength and patience, many times a day. It is joy to taste these as we receive them.

I love you and pray for you daily, Michael.

20

Dearest Kathryn,

> *I sought the Lord and he answered me*
> *and delivered me out of all my terror.*
> *Look upon Him and be radiant*
> *and let not your faces are ashamed.*
> *I called in my affliction and the Lord heard me*
> *and saved me from all my troubles.*
> *The angel of the Lord encompasses those who fear Him,*
> *and he will deliver them. Psalm 34:4-7 (The Psalter,*
> *The Book of Common Prayer)*

Terror is what we need to be delivered from, and the way to be delivered from terror is to look on the Lord. The gift of illness is that we are forced to pray and be in God's presence in the simplest way: our need is obvious and we are not capable of thoughtful prayer. So as I lay in bed sick, I couldn't help but feel I had been spread out and displayed before God. I think our first reaction is a kind of shame at being so exposed and so weak. But to know that God is regarding us in our vulnerability is also to be looking at God. To know that God sees our suffering is to begin to understand how compassion can arise – the care any of us feel when one of our own suffers. To pick up God's tender pity and to weep with Him is what makes our faces radiant, aglow with God's concern and love. To feel at our heart's depth how we and God grieve, to feel God breathe into our heart the strength and courage we need, is to find ourselves encompassed by God's protecting angel. When our trust is reduced to being simple, that clears every obstruction from our face, and they become radiant.

I love you and pray for you daily, Michael

21

Dearest Kathryn –

Save me, O God, for the waters have risen up to my neck.
I am sinking in deep mire, and there is no firm ground for
my feet.
I have come into deep waters, and the torrent washes over
me.
As for me, I am afflicted and in pain; your help, O God,
will lift me up on high.
The afflicted shall see and be glad; you who seek God,
your heart shall live. Psalm 69:1-2, 31, and 34 (The
Psalter, The Book of Common Prayer)

Even the most faithful have moments in which stable
footing is lost. We can see that old fears and physical
distress agitate parts of us: our body, whose task is to
survive, and our emotions, which blindly follow our body's
sensations and the old memories connected with them.
Like frightened children, they shake us and clutch at us,
and they can even overwhelm us, as our fears cling to us
like screaming toddlers and cause us to stumble. Our
heart's task, our soul's work, then, is to pause long enough
to see our agitation and have compassion on it, again and
again to endure with patience what our body undergoes.
Our model for this is Jesus, who from before we knew
Him, knew us with tender pity and love.

I love you and pray for you daily, Michael.

Be merciful to me, O God, be merciful to me,
 for I have taken refuge in you;
 in the shadow of your wings I take refuge
 until this time of trouble has gone by.
I cry to God Most High,
 to God who fulfills His purpose for me.
                                    Psalm 57:1-2

One translation says, "I hide under your wings until this destroying storm passes over." In those circumstances, we can't move or act. The storm is frightening and devastating. But the shadow of wings is also troubling: we may be protected, but we are also confined and smothered. No creature is meant to stay forever hidden under wings. We would not be huddled there except for the storm and the danger we are going through.

So we look at God, at the same time, with gratitude and anguish. We are protected, but not yet relieved, supported, but not removed. Of course we want to know our purpose; of course we protest. But the one constant thing, in light and dark, is God's presence and our dependence. The time of trouble shows that the one thing that cannot be removed is the fact that we and God face each other, that we have nothing effective in our hands, that our only hope is to turn to God in trust and take refuge under those wings, and in doing that, fulfill our true purpose.

I love you and pray for you daily, Michael

23

Dearest Kathryn,

> *I am grateful to God – whom I worship with a clear conscience as my ancestors did – when I remember you constantly in my prayers night and day. Recalling your tears, I long to see you, so that I may be filled with joy. I am reminded of your sincere faith, a faith that lived first in your grandmother Lois and your mother Eunice, and now, I am sure, lives in you. For this reason I remind you to rekindle the gift of God that is within you through the laying on of my hands; for God did not give us a spirit of cowardice, but rather a spirit of power and of love and of self-discipline.   II Timothy 1:3-7*

I am so glad I was able to come and visit you, to see again how much love surrounds you, to be in the presence of so much prayer. Rest in that love. Be held up by those prayers.

I love you and pray for you daily, Michael

24

Dearest Kathryn,

> *Three times I appealed to the Lord about this that it would leave me, but he said, "My grace is sufficient for you, for power is made perfect in weakness." So I will boast all the more gladly of my weakness, so that the power of Christ may dwell in me. II Corinthians 12:8-9*

The power of Christ is the power that kept Jesus faithful on the cross. The power is the unalterable grace of God that keeps us faithful as we go through what every mortal body undergoes. The power in Jesus did not prevent his death, but let the Good News he brought be known in and beyond his death.

Your witness has been your gift to me: your desire to honor God and be faithful has not wavered. You can trust that the cancer has not blocked your witness, but shown it to be true and deep, not only Christ-centered, but empowered by the grace that was in Jesus.

I love you and pray for you daily, Michael

25

Dearest Kathryn –

> *The Lord is my light and my salvation;*
> *whom shall I fear?*
> *The Lord is the stronghold of my life;*
> *of whom shall I be afraid?*
> *One thing I asked of the Lord,*
> *that will I seek after:*
> *to live in the house of the Lord*
> *all the days of my life,*
> *to behold the beauty of the Lord,*
> *and to inquire in his temple.*
>
> *Psalm 27:1, 4*

You have been brought into God's house as a dwelling place. You have made your desire to please God a steadiness in your life. You have been given a husband and children who share with you a desire to do God's will. God's love and theirs can be trusted now when you have so much pain and can do so little for yourself.

Remember that your desire to please God is God's gift to you. When you can do nothing physically, that desire to honor God is sufficient. All you need to do is rest in it, as you place your life in God's hands, over and over, and abide there.

I love you and pray for you daily, Michael

26

Dearest Kathryn –

Just as Moses lifted up the serpent in the wilderness, so must the Son of Man be lifted up, that whoever believes in him may have eternal life.

John 3:14-15.

All the people bitten by poisonous serpents needed only to look on the bronze serpent Moses made in order to be restored. Jesus presents himself as what we are to look at now.

As you can, when you can, remember that all you need to do is lift your eyes to Jesus, hanging on the cross, sharing your suffering, suffering with you and for you. Those outstretched arms receive and lift and carry you. Place yourself in them over and over.

I love you and pray for you daily, Michael

27

Dearest Kathryn –

> *How dear to me is your dwelling, O Lord of Hosts!*
> *My soul has a desire and longing for the courts of the Lord;*
> *My heart and my flesh rejoice in the Living God.*
> *The sparrow has found her a house, and the swallow a nest*
>   *where she may lay her young:*
> *By the side of your altars, O Lord of Hosts,*
>   *my King and my God. Psalm 84:1-2 (The Psalter, The*
> *Book of Common Prayer)*

When I think of you, I know how true these verses are for you. All your life you have known this longing, and throughout your life you have made God's courts your home. You have laid your young by God's altars. Honoring God has been your journey.

Now that illness has broken up the ability of heart and flesh to rejoice in the simple and obvious blessings, remember your longing for God. Desiring healing and release from suffering are natural and urgent, but they are temporary and circumstantial. Hold on to the longing for God that has been yours all your life. Reduce it to its essence. Return again and again to the simple love of God. Do not be afraid to climb up on those altars and offer yourself as well completely in that love where God dwells.

I love you and pray for you daily, Michael

28

Dearest Kathryn –

> *Happy are the people, whose strength is in God,*
> *whose hearts are set on the pilgrim way!*
> *When they go through the desolate valley,*
> *they will find it a place of springs,*
> *for the early rains have covered it with pools of water.*
> *They will climb from height to height,*
> *And the God of gods will reveal himself in Zion.*
> *Psalm 84:5-7 (The Psalter, The Book of Common Prayer)*

Dear sister, your heart has been set on the pilgrim way all your life. This stretch, this desolate valley, is so hard, and it hurts me so to see you suffer. The journey of the pilgrim is a journey of the heart. Each moment the awareness of God returns to you, you can hold it and look at it. Take deep breaths, because, as they open your lungs, they remind you to open yourself, to draw God in, so that God becomes the breath inside your breath. These moments are the pools of water in the desolate valley. Drink God in slowly and deeply, and feel Him, like cold water, moving into you as your strength and comfort. God is with us always, but we need over and over to pause and focus on Him and open to Him. Each of those moments is a climb to another height as our heart journeys to God, our companion and our goal.

I love you and pray for you daily, Michael

29

Dearest Kathryn –

> *The angel said to Mary, "Nothing will be impossible for God."*
>
> *And Mary said, "Here am I, the servant of the Lord; let it be with me according to your word." Then the angel departed from her. Luke 1:37-38*

In the stillness of God's deep arrival in us, all we need to do is turn and say "yes." The greatest spiritual challenge is to make a gift of what is inevitable. It is easy to say 'yes" when we have freedom of movement and the sense that we can act to adjust what we receive from God's hands. It is hard to say "yes" when we know what is being given has no room for our reservations and accommodations. What we have left with us always is the power to say "yes." What we always have is our power to consent. It takes strong will to unclench and relax our hands, but there is peace in saying "yes." I believe we can only do it with God's help and in God's presence, since only God can receive the final "yes" when we hand over all we are. Each day, learning to say "yes" over and over, to say "yes" more and more fully, we give our self through our life to God.

I love you and pray for you daily, Michael.

30

Dearest Kathryn,

> *Hearken to my voice, O Lord, when I call;*
> *Have mercy on me and answer me.*
> *You speak in my heart and say,*
>   *"Seek my face."*
> *Your face, O Lord, will I seek.*
> *Psalm 27:10-11 (The Psalter, The Book of*
> *Common Prayer)*

All that is necessary is to listen for the voice of God in you now. It is still and small, beneath your heartbeat. Listen to your heart beating; the voice of God can be heard between the beats, continuous. That is the voice that will remain when all our heartbeats have stopped, from everlasting to everlasting. It says, "I sustain you, I love you, seek me; you will find me, because I am never absent from you; I do not abandon you, because I have been with you every day of your life; turn to me and learn of me, because I love you." The silence between our heartbeats is the voice of God, never abandoning us, always beneath us and within us, holding us up. All we need to do is turn to it, seek it, lean on it, knowing that within it, carrying us is God, who is Love.

I love you and pray for you daily, Michael

31

Dearest Kathryn –

> *For God alone my soul in silence waits;*
>   *from him comes my salvation.*
> *He alone is my rock and my salvation,*
>   *my stronghold, so that I shall not be greatly shaken.*
> *Psalm 62:1-2 (The Psalter, The Book of Common Prayer)*

When I was in intensive care, I was barely able to speak, and the effort of figuring out words was too much. I felt afloat, barely in my body. My illness had become me entirely. That silence was forced on me.

But in the silence forced on me, I discovered the silence occupying me. Part of me was still alert and noticing things and aware of myself, and that part noticed the deep silence that is always with me. That silence always waits for God; it watches with hope. All we need to do is sit there to understand that we have longed for God all our life. It is the one solid thing. When we can do no more, we lean back into the silence within us and wait for God, and God, who sustains us all our life, does not fail to meet us there.

I love you and pray for you daily, Michael

Dearest Kathryn –

> *O God, You are my God; eagerly I seek You.*
> *My soul thirsts for You, my flesh faints for You,*
> *   as in a barren and dry land where there is no water.*
> *Therefore I have gazed upon You in Your holy place,*
> *   that I might behold Your power and Your glory.*
> *For Your loving-kindness is better than life itself;*
> *   My lips shall give You praise. Psalm 63:1-3 (The Psalter,*
> *The Book of Common Prayer)*

How well the Psalmist says everything that needs to be said! We come to understand our thirst as we learn over and over that the deepest contentment and peace came to us as we drank from God. You can use the memory of that to steady you now. Our desire for God was given to us by God, and to be in touch with that is to be in touch, not with our fallenness, but with our homing instinct. When we long for God, we are not lost, we are oriented. God enables our gaze – to know we look for God and thirst for Him is to know one of His gifts, to know His activity in our life, to know Him finally. Within our suffering, that homing instinct cannot be taken away. Only fear can block and bury it. But God's loving-kindness is greater. If we relax our grip, He has given us what will lead us to Him

I love you and pray for you daily, Michael

Dearest Kathryn –

> *I remember You upon my bed*
> *and meditate on you in the night watches.*
> *You have been my helper,*
> *and under the shadow of Your wings,*
> *I will rejoice.*
> *My soul clings to you; your right hand holds me fast.*
> *Psalm 63:6-8 (The Psalter, The Book of Common Prayer*

As God comes to mind, turn your thoughts there. Hold your attention on the One who hovers over you to comfort and protect you. Our energy and ability to focus will rise and fall, but to God, who watches us tenderly always, we are like children. Our wandering and waiting are occasions for God's affection and compassion to move even more close to us and take us up in His arms.

Your work is to rest there. That is all you have to do: to lean back against God and be held and show Him where it hurts.

I love you and pray for you daily. Michael

34

Dearest Kathryn –

> *As the deer longs for the water-brooks,*
>   *so longs my soul for you, O God;*
> *My soul is athirst for God, athirst for the living God.*
> *When shall I come to appear before the presence of God?*
> *My tears have been my food day and night,*
>   *while all day long they say to me,*
> *"Where now is your God?"*
> *I pour out my soul when I think of these things;*
>   *how I went with the multitude*
>   *and led them into the house of God,*
>   *with the voice of praise and thanksgiving,*
>   *among those who keep holy-day.*
> *Why are you so full of heaviness, O my soul?*
> *Why are you so disquieted within me?*
> *Put your trust in God,*
>   *for I will yet give thanks to Him,*
>   *who is the help of my countenance and my God.*
> *Psalm 42:1-7* (The Psalter, The Book of Common Prayer0

You are not alone in your longing for God, nor in your readiness to give thanks.

I love you and pray for you daily, Michael

35

Dearest Kathryn –

> *Jesus looked up to heaven and said, "Father, the hour has come; glorify your Son so that the Son may glorify You, since You have given Him authority over all people, to give eternal life to all whom You have given him. And this is eternal life that they may know You, the only true God, and Jesus Christ, whom You have sent. I glorified You on earth by finishing the work You gave me to do." John 17:1-4*

After the Last Supper, Jesus prayed for his disciples. The finishing of our work is always prayer. What we do is never finished: there is always some loose thread, some new turn. Only time moves some things past us and they are finished for us then. But our last words, our finishing our task, are our prayer: putting what we have in God's hands. Particularly with those we love, we do not want to be finished. By praying for them, by putting them in God's hands and leaving them there, we do not finish with them, because in God nothing ever ends. It takes all our faith to hand what we care about to God and know we will find those we love again in Him

I love you and pray for you daily. Michael

36

Dearest Kathryn –

> *Jesus prayed, "I have made Your Name known to those whom You gave me from the world. They were yours, and You gave them to me, and they have kept your word. Now they know that everything You have given me is from You, for the words that You gave to me I have given to them.. "*
> *John 17:6-8a*

Jesus' words about himself and his disciples also have a way of being true about us as his followers. The Holy Spirit enables us in lesser ways to do what He did. I think often of the way the Spirit led you "into all truth" and of the truths to which you made your life faithful. You made God's Name known by the way you built your entire life around your whole-hearted intention to give God honor and glory. Those of us whom God gave you, particularly David and your children, who always belong to God, have been witnesses of your devotion and faithfulness all the way to this day. You have fulfilled everything: you have given witness to God every day. No other work is needed, because those you love already remain in God's hands.

I love you and pray for you daily, Michael

37

Dearest Kathryn –

> *Jesus prayed and said, "I am asking on their behalf; I am not asking on behalf of the world, but on behalf of those whom You gave me, because they are yours. And now I am no longer in the world, but they are in the world, and I am coming to You. Holy Father, protect them in Your Name that You have given me, so that they may be one as we are one. Now I am coming to You, and I speak these things in the world, so that they may have my joy made complete in themselves." John 17: 9, 11, 13*

It seems to me that Jesus shows us how to take leave. The same God that holds us holds those we love. Our concerns with the world fall away and final prayers are for what we love, for those whom we love, for those whose story is also our story. But, as Jesus says, we can only take leave if we know that they belong, first and always, to God. The people we love belong to God; they are God's all along, who gave them to us. But if they belong to God, as we do, they are protected and safe. They are already held as one in the very place that we have our final home, where we also are headed. That we are all one is the joy nothing can take away.

I love you and pray for you daily, Michael.

38

Dearest Kathryn –

> *Jesus prayed for his disciples and said, "For their sakes, I sanctify myself, so that they may also be sanctified in truth. Father, I desire that these also, whom you have given men, may be with me where I am, to see my glory, which You have given me because You loved me before the foundation of the world. I made Your Name known to them, and I will make it known, so that the love with which You have loved me may be in them, and I in them." John 17: 19, 24, 26*

Once we know God's love, we know what it is like to be loved from before the foundation of the world, a love that the accidents and incidents of the world don't change. It is not God's love if it changes. We only need to know it and rest in it and let it change us. All those we care about are loved in the same way. We cannot provide for them more than God already has. God loves them as He loves us, and His love abides in them as it does in us. God will bring them to know that love as He brought us; and the love we have known will also be known, by God's grace, to them. Always what we hope is already in God's hands. To finish our work, we only need to trust that Truth.

I love you and pray for you daily, Michael

39

Dearest Kathryn –

I still my soul and make it quiet,
like a child upon its mother's breast;
my soul is quieted within me.
O Israel, wait on the Lord
from this time forth and for evermore.

Psalm 131:3-4

When I was on the edge of going into a coma, I found myself sinking into enforced stillness, unable to talk or move effectively. After the period of struggle, all I could do was lie there. I found then an attention that came and went, but that was at peace, and more and more I felt myself being held up by God. For you also, I know those arms are the same. Lean back into them and let your soul be at rest there, where you are sustained and cared for, from which we drink all the endurance and patience and acceptance we have. Waiting quietly for God's grace is already a grace received.

I love you and pray for you daily, Michael

40

Dearest Kathryn –

> *To You I lift up my eyes,*
> *to You enthroned in the heavens.*
> *As the eyes of servants*
> *look to the hands of their masters,*
> *and the eyes of a maid to the hand of her*
> *mistress,*
> *So our eyes look to the Lord, our God,*
> *until He shows us His mercy.*

Psalm 123:1-3(The Psalter, The Book of Common Prayer)

Steadiness of vision is all. None of us, I believe, likes to think of our self so at the disposal of another, and we can react with anger. But the accomplishment is to choose what is inevitable, to consent whole-heartedly to what is unavoidable, and to keep our eye on our master's hand, that is, on what is given to us each day. Our peace lies in seeing it without judgment and responding to it with simple faithfulness each day. Our part is to say, "I will not look away, I will not remove myself, I will remain in your presence, I will wait on You." That remains in our hands always.

I love you and pray for you daily, Michael

41

Dearest Kathryn –

> *See, the home of God is with mortals; He will dwell among them as their God, and they will be His people, God Himself will be with them He will wipe every tear from their eyes. Death will be no more; mourning and crying and pain will be no more, for the first things have passed away. Revelation 21:3-4*

The promises of God are sure. God dwells in us as a pledge that we will dwell in God. What has impeded our clear sight will be gone, and the peace and joy we have known here, as reflections on water in a swift-flowing stream, will be our home. All that has caused us trouble will be no more, and what we have lived for will be ours.

Turn that way, where love waits for you.

I love you and pray for you daily, Michael

42

Dearest Kathryn –

> *I love the Lord, because He has heard*
> *the voice of my supplication,*
> *because He has inclined His ear to me*
> *whenever I called upon Him.*
> *The cords of death entangled me;*
> *the grip of the grave took hold of me;*
> *I came to grief and sorrow.*
> *Then I called upon the name of the Lord:*
> *"O Lord, I pray you, save my life."*
>
> *Gracious is our God and righteous;*
> *the Lord is full of compassion.*
> *The Lord watches over the innocent;*
> *I was brought very low and He helped me.*
>
> *Turn again to your rest, O my soul,*
> *for the Lord has treated you well.*
>
> *You have rescued my life from death,*
> *my eyes from tears, my feet from stumbling.*
> *I will walk in the presence of the Lord*
> *in the land of the living.*
> *Psalm 116:1-9* (The Psalter, The Book of Common
> Prayer)

If we had no faith, these words would be cruel. But we know that the land of the living is not confined to our bodies, and I know your love of God, and I believe that your soul is kept safe in God, where there are no tears or stumbling.

Turn to your rest, then walk in the land of the living.

I love you and pray for you daily, Michael

43

Dearest Kathryn –

> *When the Lord restored the fortunes of Zion,*
>   *then we were like those who dream;*
>   *then was our mouth filled with laughter*
>   *and our tongue with shouts of joy;*
>   *then they said among the nations,*
> *"The Lord has done great things for them."*
> *The Lord has done great things for us,*
>   *and we are glad indeed.*
>
> *Restore our fortunes, O Lord,*
>   *like the watercourses of the Negev.*
> *Those who sowed with tears*
>   *will reap with songs of joy.*
> *Those who went out weeping,*
>   *carrying their seed,*
>   *will come again rejoicing,*
>   *shouldering their sheaves.*
> *Psalm 126 (The Psalter, The Book of Common Prayer)*

When I read this Psalm to you and you could barely speak, even then you murmured agreement and nodded your head. The Lord has done great things in you. Listen for the songs of joy in you even now.

I love you and pray for you daily, Michael

44

Dearest Kathryn –

What then are we to say about these things? If God is for us, who can be against us? He who did not withhold His own Son, but gave Him up for all of us, will He not with Him also give us everything else? Who will bring any charge against God's elect? It is God who justifies. Who is to condemn? It is Christ Jesus, who died, yes, who was raised, who is at the right hand of God, who intercedes for us.

What will separate us from the love of Christ? Will hardship, or distress, or persecution, or famine, or nakedness, or peril, or sword? As it is written,

"For Your sake we are being killed all the day long; we are accounted as sheep to be slaughtered."

No; in all these things, we are more than conquerors through Him who loved us. For I am convinced that neither death, nor life, nor angels, nor rulers, nor things present, nor things to come, nor powers, nor height, nor depth, nor anything else in all creation, will be able to separate us from the love of God in Christ Jesus our Lord. Romans 8:31-39

I love you and pray for you daily, Michael

45

Dearest Kathryn –

> *How precious is your steadfast love, O God!*
> *All people may take refuge under the shadow of Your*
>   *wings.*
> *They feast on the abundance of Your house,*
>   *and You give them drink from the river of Your*
>   *delights.*
> *For in You is the fountain of life;*
>   *and in Your light, we see light.*
> *Psalm 36:7-9 (The Psalter, The Book of Common Prayer)*

Drink deeply from God-in-you.

Offer yourself into the light.

I love you and pray for you daily, Michael

46

Dearest Kathryn –

> *You, who live in the shelter of the Most High,*
> *Who abide in the shadow of the Almighty,*
>   *will say to the Lord,*
>   *"My refuge, my fortress, my God in whom I trust."*
> *He will deliver you from the snare of the fowler*
>   *and from deadly pestilence.*
> *He will give His angels charge over you*
>   *to guard you in all your ways.*
> *They will bear you up on their hands,*
>   *so that you will not dash your foot against a stone.*
> *Psalm 91:1-3, 11-12 (The Psalter, The Book of Common*
> *Prayer)*

Look at Jesus, your refuge, and send your heart to Him. You are being carried over by prayers and powers. Place yourself in Christ's light and fall asleep there where you are held.

I love you and pray for you daily, Michael

POS DATA

Kathryn died on March 26. This letter was written to her family from Michael.

Martha said to Jesus,

"Lord, if you had been here my brother would not have died. But even now I know that God will give you whatever you ask."

Jesus said to her, "Your brother will rise again."

Martha said to him, "I know that he will rise again in the resurrection on the last day."

Jesus said to her, "I am the Resurrection and the Life. Those who believe on me, even though they die, will live, and everyone who lives and believes in me will never die. Do you believe this?"

She said to him, "Yes, Lord, I believe that you are the Messiah, the Son of God, and the one coming into the world."

John 11:21-27

31 March, 2003

Dear David, Jonathan, Daniel, Charlotte, Stephen, Nathan, Andrew and Karen –

I have been thinking so much about all of you in these days and praying for you. Before leaving Knoxville, I went out to the cemetery and saw Kathryn's fresh grave and thought again about her courage and faithfulness and love.

Such a great gift of grace, when it is taken from us, must leave an enormous and uneraseable sense of loss. I believe our love of Kathryn will continue to find expression in a sense that what has left us has left us with no replacement possible, with a gap no other human being can fill. That seems to me proper, a way of acknowledging before God Kathryn's uniqueness as His child. It is right to grieve that.

I know also that your faith is your consolation in these days. Your conviction that Kathryn already rejoices in God's light will also comfort you as you affirm that you will come to share that light with her one day and be with her in glory. May that comfort fill you.

In the days to come, all of you will have opportunities over and over to bring Kathryn's love back into your family. You children, as you look at each other, still see Kathryn's flesh; she made you out of her body, so, in a sense, you will be one way in which she is still with you. I pray that that will be more than a physical trace and be also a spiritual legacy, so that the love she felt – and still feels - for all of you will find expression in the way you care for each other.

You are all in my prayers.   Michael

REMEMBRANCE OF KATHRYN
Words spoken at her funeral by her brother, Michael

It would be difficult, for anyone looking in at this event from the outside to believe that grief is not the only thing we feel here, but also gratitude. I still cannot grasp the size of this loss and how it will change all of us for good. Watching Kathryn suffer was wrenching and numbing. And yet, in all of it, I cannot help but hear the words of the Book of Revelation, "to the one that is faithful unto death, I will give the crown of life."

I will not speak about my relationship with my sister, but about her testimony. Early in the days of her illness, I recall that she said that her fear was that she would not remain a faithful witness: that as the cancer took over, she would become someone she did not want to be, someone who would not bring honor to her Lord. She was afraid that she would lose control of her speech and use language she abhorred. She was afraid she would lose control of her emotions and become bitter or angry. She was afraid she would despair and lose her faith.

Her Christian dedication had prepared her for the work she then took on. If we say that our life of discipleship is about giving ourselves to Christ, then illness is a moment in which the promise we made can be made good. Over the years she was sick, she examined herself and probed herself, cleaning out what stood in the way, preparing herself for the miracle of healing. She reviewed past actions and present attitudes, and every sport of rust was scoured away for God's sake.

Nor was it all a matter of introspection. She also looked around her to those whom she met in hospitals and treatment centers, and paused to hear their story and to share hers, to testify to the gifts of grace she had received, to call their attention to the hope in their life, and often to pray with them. In this way, she continued to purge and strengthen her own faith, to see for herself the gifts she received from God, to awaken her own thanksgiving. She made sure, during her illness, to work on our parents' fiftieth wedding anniversary celebration, giving it a sweet shape that was entirely her own stamp. It seems to me that Debbi and I simply helped her bring it about. She was at a reception in Washington, DC, and met a couple, both of whom were cancer survivors. As their conversation came to an end, she asked if she could pray for them – and she did, unashamed to show her simple faith and generous gratitude, while oblivious chatter went on around them. The couple later told me no one had prayed for them like that before.

Her life was a powerful testimony to God's sustaining grace. Her lesson for us is this simple and comprehensive way of giving herself, that is, of loving: of loving others so much that she was always attentive and of loving God so much that she was never ashamed. As she came to grasp the length of the final journey she was on, her self-examination and faithfulness moved from being the groundwork for a miracle to becoming the deeper work of placing everything in God's hands. This is a difficult lesson for us human beings: we are often good, expecting rewards. But I believe Kathryn passed beyond that and found that giving herself was sufficient, and all had been given to One who is able to keep that which we have committed to Him against the day. Her self-offering now had no other purpose than devotion. The greatest challenge we face as mortal creatures is how to turn the inevitable into a free gift, how not to resent our fate, how to turn our death into the last and fullest expression of our self. She was ready for that.

I had a glimpse of this when I asked her one day if she wanted me to read to her. At that point in the cancer's progression, she could not longer see clearly, and the structure and meaning of the printed word were out of her reach. Instantly, she went and got her Bible and asked for the Psalms to be read. From her childhood she had memorized Scripture, and now even beloved verses were not returning to her. She asked me simply to read where I could see that she had marked verses, these were the ones she had earlier memorized and wanted to have present to her again. So I did. Too much had, by then, been cut away from her, and the words she loved did not return as familiar friends: she listened and said they were wonderful, but over and over said she just couldn't remember them.

But even in this, her depth of faith and her love of God caused her to reach for what she heard, yes, with puzzled regret at her loss, but still with amazed joy. The Bible became, in a sense, fresh to her again. Scripture took on new depth. She was hearing as if for the first time the reassurances of the God she trusted, and she recognized, if not the words, the love. She would sit in her chair, and later lie in her bed, and she would echo some of the words, or say, "Oh, yes," or "thank you." As speaking became more difficult, she would simply make little sounds of appreciation and gratitude, as if listening to the words of a love-letter. When I was last with her, early this month, I reread to her a Psalm I had read months before, a Psalm that she had marked over nearly in its entirety. As I read it, during the whole time, she murmured agreement and smiled. This is that Psalm

When the Lord restored the fortunes of Zion,
Then were we like those who dream.
Then was our mouth filled with laughter
And our tongue with shouts of joy.
Then they said among the nations,

" The Lord has done great things for them!"
The Lord has done great things for us,
and we are glad indeed.
Those who sow with tears
will reap with songs of joy.
Those who went out weeping, carrying their seed,
Will come again with joy, shouldering their sheaves.

May we all learn to shoulder our sheaves with the joy and faith Kathryn had.

To close, I will use a prayer from the Burial Office of the Episcopal Church. Please join me. Let us pray.

"Into your hands, O merciful Savior, we commend your servant Kathryn. Acknowledge, we humbly beseech you, a sheep of your own fold, a lamb of your own flock, a sinner of your own redeeming. Receive her into the arms of your mercy, into the blessed rest of everlasting peace, and into the glorious company of the saints in light. Amen."

**Letter written to Kathryn from Michael at her request
to know what it was like to be in a coma**

10 December, 2002

Dearest Kathryn –

I am sorry this letter is so long. Maybe David or Mother
or Daddy can read it to you in sections.

I am so grateful for the times we have had to read
Scripture together. The Psalms are able to say things we
cannot find words for. I am moved knowing they are
God's words given to us to use in prayer and praise of
Him – God giving us His own words to use as we
approach Him. I am humbled when I realize that Jesus
himself knew these words and used then when he prayed
and sang God's praise, and that we can say these words
with him. Now you and I have been able to join him in
the same words he said. And I will mark in my Prayer
book Psalm 16 as the Psalm of promise in your illness.

I particularly wanted to write because you asked me
something as we walked Sunday morning that I later
thought I didn't answer very well, so I wanted to write to
answer you more fully. You asked me if I had gone into a
coma when I had meningitis and what that was like. I
didn't go into a coma, but I was very close. According to
my doctor, I was actually in the early stages of dying when
they caught and began to treat the illness. I think you
wanted to know something about that, so I am writing you
to tell you a little more about it.

What I remember most about the time before going to the
Emergency Room was the terrible pain. I have never hurt
so much. My head ached and all my joints. My hands

were so cramped that I could not lift the bedcovers over myself, because I couldn't get my fingers to close on them and grip them enough to lift them and pull them.

But in that much pain, a strange thing happened. I found that I had a kind of patience and endurance and strength I didn't know I had. The body can withstand more than I thought. Since there was no way to put any of this down, I found that the pain and I were holding each other. I do not know how else to put it. I was definitely in the grip of the pain and couldn't escape, but the pain was also something that I was holding and watching, something that I was holding in my attention. I saw, from a very calm place, that my hands didn't work, that I couldn't straighten my joints, but that this was OK, somehow I myself was not at risk, not in danger. Like I say, I was surprised by my patience. I knew that, one way or another, the pain would end, and all I needed to do in the mean time was to be patient and to watch it. Robin Moore, my friend, was sleeping in the next room, to look after me during the night, if I needed anything. (Her husband was upstairs. I had gone to visit them on Sunday and first felt symptoms during supper – chills & trembling.) I knew that I didn't want to trouble her, because she could do nothing about the pain. So I also understood there was nothing to do about this and no point in demanding things of other people who couldn't help. So I found that my patience was extended into not whining or protesting or complaining or demanding. I believe you are already living through some of the same things.

In the morning, Robin and her husband took me to the Emergency Room. I think these are the important things to tell you. I was still in terrible pain. I couldn't walk and could not sign my name for the consent forms. But through the pain, I was aware of what was going on around me. I understood the questions I was asked and knew where I was. I knew the answer to the questions, but couldn't speak. My head was hanging down on my chest, and I could only nod it to answer questions. If I moved at all, it was very slowly, with a lot of effort and pain. They said on the admission forms I was disoriented and lethargic, but I was not disoriented, only unable to communicate, and I was lethargic because I could hardly move. I began to feel that I was in something like a glass case. I could see out of it and hear through it, but I couldn't move or speak through it. It felt like I had taken a step backwards out of my body that I had begun to separate out of it, that it was in front of me, but no longer fully part of me. My doctor told me later that this sense of separation is one of the first stages of dying that sense of pulling backwards out of the body. It was not painful or frightening – only something I noticed. Like I said, the only feeling I had was of pain everywhere and my own endurance of it.

I had other sensations, too. When I was in the Intensive Care Unit, most of the time I felt like I was floating. I wasn't clear what direction was up; I thought at one point the bed was standing on end and that the ceiling was a wall that I was facing. Another time I thought I was hanging upside down. This was not a sensation of falling, only a loss of my sense of direction. I saw flashes of light and odd shapes, mostly red, squirming and shifting. Patches of my field of vision went away. It was as if someone had taken what I could see and torn a piece out of it or cracked it, so that what I saw had a tear in it, at moments through the broken section of the field of vision, it looked as if I could see light coming through, other times it looked liked nothing, simply a missing place out of what I could see.

I felt like I was floating on a deep lake and that my face was exactly at the surface, but about to sink under. It was not frightening, only heavy and still. It was a little like going to sleep, but not exactly because I had no sense of the rest of my body. It felt like all but my face had already sunk beneath the surface of this lake, only my face was out of the water and that was all that I had a physical sensation of. (One of the nurses would come in and talk to me and stroke my arm and ask me very simple questions about my life – Were my parents alive? Where did they live? -- and these questions would pull me back up to the surface, where I would answer, then begin to sink down again. I thank she was checking to make sure I was still alert, but what mattered most to me was that I was being reminded over and over that I had a life and a story. I came to believe that those questions kept me in the world, as I remembered who I am.)

The most important thing to say is that none of this was frightening. I was aware that I was being held. I felt God's arms underneath me and underneath everything that was happening to me. I did not feel them as physical arms, not as a physical holding, but as deep steadiness and reassurance, though truly beneath me supporting me. I felt I was being held up through it all, but also that I could lean back and rest on those arms and that I was safe there. I did not have a sense of being visited by Jesus or God, only that God was underneath me, holding it all up, totally faithful and trustworthy. All I had to do was agree to hand over my spirit at the right moment, which was not yet there, but I could feel myself leaning back into it and sinking down towards it. There, the promises are sure.

I am so grateful for your faithful witness through your illness. It seems to me that you have trusted God at each step and as Job, did not sin with your mouth, but continued to accept the good and the bad. Our faith is most precious when it is tried as silver is tried. I can certainly testify that God is ensuring that all things are working together for good in this, because your testimony continues to give God praise and to trust God's goodness. The steadiness of your faith, even as you have moments of doubt, is the good that God is bringing about. The doubts hardly matter, because the result is that you return each time to God, reaffirming your love and devotion and commitment. Whatever test you go through, you return with praise and trust to the Lord that cares for you and calls you to follow Him where He leads. I find my own faith strengthened by your witness, so that is another good that God is causing to work here and that I am receiving from God through you. Miracles are not necessary, because the deeper good is that your tested faith remains sure; the good is that you are unswervingly loyal to the One who already has redeemed you and blessed you and sanctified you. You have not made your love conditional on your physical healing, but have continued to praise and trust Him.

Remember that all that will be required of you is to continue to trust God and to place more and more in Jesus' compassionate hands. As your adult self-reliance falls away, each part can be placed with a thank-you in God's loving hands. You already know that, and I hardly feel I have any right to say these things, because you are living them, but I want to reassure you and encourage you, to affirm what I see you doing. The independence of being able to drive or teaching the children of your body that you love so much -- both those are gifts that you have already handed over into God's hands with a thank-you that you had the opportunity to do them for a while. Each child now needs lovingly to be put in God's trustworthy hands. And now, reading and writing are put in God's hands, with thanks for being able to use those skills for a while.

We become more like children when we are sick. As you have become more like a child in your skill level and in your inability to act independently, your trust and love is more apparent and stronger. Children, because they depend on adults, trust more deeply than adults who learn to be self-reliant. And, just as children's trust and love doesn't depend on their being able to read or to speak, only on the fullness of their heart and their love of those who care for them, so you are able to become like the little children who are whatever it is that you happen to have at any moment. We can love with all our fullness, whatever we are filled with, even if it is less than we had at one time and less than we wish we could offer.

Of course, finally, everything we have and are will be returned to God, and for each thing, we need to say thanks as we return it to God. At the end, all we have to do is hand our life back to God without any reservation at all, and with thanks for all the blessings we have received and with hope for the greater blessings of heaven. We have deserved none of these blessings, except for God's extravagant grace, and we can claim no hope except for the merits of Jesus Christ, who died for us and who has already shown us the way to Resurrection.

I love you very much and I thank God for the gift of these last few days we were together.

I pray for you daily. Michael.

MICHAEL WYATT
August 27, 1951-July 7, 2009

The Rev. Dr. Michael Wyatt, Episcopal priest, died of liver cancer at the age of 57. The son of missionary parents, he grew up in Spain, Chile and Colombia. After serving as director of a bilingual school in Cali, Colombia, he earned a Masters of Divinity with distinction in 1985 from the Church Divinity School of the Pacific, Berkley, California. Following ordination to the priesthood, he served churches in the San Francisco area. He received his Ph. D. from Emory University in 1996, writing a dissertation on the theological validity of the claims about God made in Alcoholics Anonymous and other Twelve Step Programs.

In Seattle he served as the Dean of the Diocesan School of Ministry and Theology and the Associate Rector of St. Stephen's Church. In 2001 he moved to Washington DC. to be the Canon Theologian at Washington National Cathedral, focusing on interfaith theological work, Scriptural scholarship and current developments in Christian theology. In 2006 he moved to St. Cloud, Minnesota, to serve as priest to St. John's Episcopal Church and as Adjunct professor at St. Cloud State University.

People who knew Michael marveled at his ability to synthesize complex concepts and to educate in a loving and affirming manner to any level of listener. He had a quick wit, a quick smile and a love for beauty. He combined his love of God and his love of the outdoors while making his pilgrimage on the El Camino a Santiago de Campostela, Spain. He was an accomplished musician. Several of his compositions were performed at his memorial service at St. Stephen's Episcopal Church, Seattle, Washington, where his remains are in the Columbarium.